Field Day!

Represent and Interpret Data

Cindy D'Anna

ROSEN
COMMON CORE MATH
READERS

Rosen
Classroom™

New York

Published in 2014 by The Rosen Publishing Group, Inc.
29 East 21st Street, New York, NY 10010

Book Design: Jon D'Rozario

D'Anna, Cindy.
Field day!: represent and interpret data / by Cindy D'Anna.
  p. cm. — (Core math skills: measurement and geometry)
Includes index.
ISBN 978-1-4777-2229-9 (library binding)
ISBN 978-1-4777-2046-2 (pbk.)
ISBN 978-1-4777-2047-9 (6-pack)
1. Mathematical statistics — Juvenile literature. I. Title.
QA276.3 D36 2014
519.5—d23

Manufactured in the United States of America

CPSIA Compliance Information: Batch #CS13RC: For further information contact Rosen Publishing, New York, New York at 1-800-237-9932.

Word Count: 385

Contents

Playing Games

It's Field Day at my school! We get to play outside all day. There are a lot of fun sports and games for us to play. I can't wait to play with my friends. It's my **favorite** day of the year!

5

Kickball

We play kickball first. Our class breaks up into different groups. The red team has 12 kids. The blue team has 11. My teacher makes 2 kids be the **referees**. Which group has the most kids? The red team has the most kids.

number of kids

15
14
13
12
11
10
9
8
7
6
5
4
3
2
1

red team   blue team   referee

group

7

There are boys and girls in every group. Which group has the most boys? The red team has 5 boys. The blue team has 8 boys. There's 1 boy referee. The blue team has the most boys.

number
of boys

15
14
13
12
11
10
9
8
7
6
5
4
3
2
1

red team   blue team   referee

group

9

Which group has the most girls? The red team has 7 girls. The blue team has 3 girls. There's 1 girl referee. The red team has the most girls, because 7 is greater than both 3 and 1.

	red team	blue team	referee
girls	7	3	1

> < =
greater than | less than | equal to

$7 > 3 > 1$

Water Balloon Toss

Next, we do a water balloon toss. It's really fun! There are 10 green water balloons and 7 purple water balloons. There are 5 pink water balloons, too. There are fewer pink balloons than other colors.

We have 22 water balloons. There are 13 big balloons and 9 small balloons. What do we have more of—big or small? Since 13 is greater than 9, we have more big water balloons.

big   small

13 > 9

Running a Race

Next, we run a race. Who runs the fastest? Kyle runs the race in 38 seconds. Alyssa runs the race in 41 seconds. I run the race in 45 seconds. Kyle runs fastest, because 38 seconds is less than 41 seconds. It's less than 45 seconds, too.

Kyle   Alyssa   Me

0:38   0:41   0:45

38 < 41 < 45

17

Ring Toss

My friends and I do a ring toss. Whoever gets the most rings around the **cone** wins. Carson gets 2 rings. Molly gets 4 rings. I get 6 rings. I win the ring toss because 6 is greater than 4. It's also greater than 2.

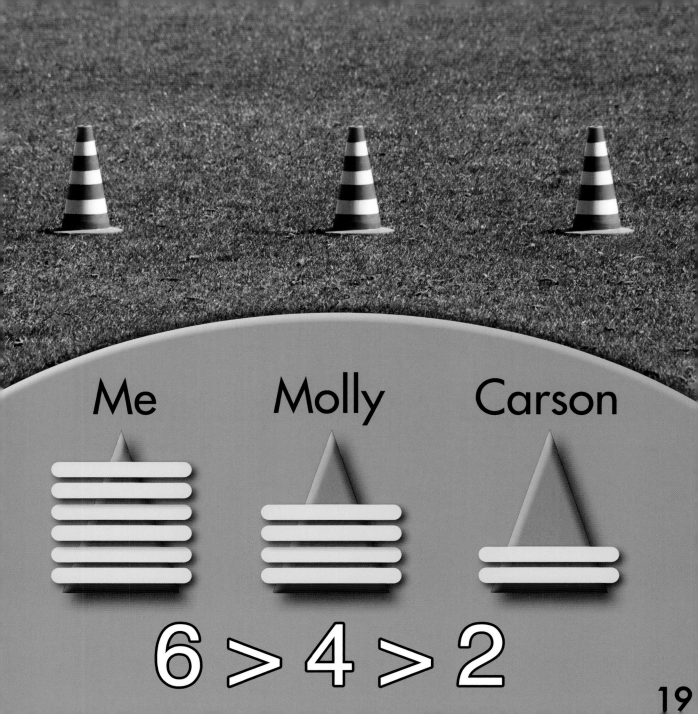

Me   Molly   Carson

6 > 4 > 2

Healthy Snacks

Exercising makes us very hungry! There are 3 kinds of fruit for us to eat. There are 10 bananas, 10 oranges, and 10 apples. Each group has 10 fruits in it. That means the groups are equal.

bananas   oranges   apples

10 = 10 = 10

Lots of Fun

Field Day was a lot of fun! I'm tired from exercising so much. Does your school have a field day? What's your favorite thing to do?

Glossary

cone (KOHN) A shape with a round bottom and a point at the top.

favorite (FAY-vuh-ruht) Liked best.

referee (reh-fuh-REE) Somebody who makes sure everyone follows the rules of a game.

Index

Due to the changing nature of Internet links, The Rosen Publishing Group, Inc., has developed an online list of websites related to the subject of this book. This site is updated regularly. Please use this link to access the list: www.powerkidslinks.com/cms/mg/fda